YOUR KNOWLEDGE HAS VALUE

AF150144

- We will publish your bachelor's and master's thesis, essays and papers

- Your own eBook and book - sold worldwide in all relevant shops

- Earn money with each sale

Upload your text at www.GRIN.com and publish for free

Anonym

Human Side of Innovation. A Short Discussion of Four Studies

GRIN Publishing

Bibliographic information published by the German National Library:

The German National Library lists this publication in the National Bibliography; detailed bibliographic data are available on the Internet at http://dnb.dnb.de .

Imprint:

Copyright © 2014 GRIN Verlag GmbH
Print and binding: Books on Demand GmbH, Norderstedt Germany
ISBN: 978-3-656-86042-6

This book at GRIN:

http://www.grin.com/en/e-book/285767/human-side-of-innovation-a-short-discussion-of-four-studies

GRIN - Your knowledge has value

Since its foundation in 1998, GRIN has specialized in publishing academic texts by students, college teachers and other academics as e-book and printed book. The website www.grin.com is an ideal platform for presenting term papers, final papers, scientific essays, dissertations and specialist books.

Visit us on the internet:

http://www.grin.com/

http://www.facebook.com/grincom

http://www.twitter.com/grin_com

Discussion of Four Research Studies and Four Case Studies within the Seminar in "The Human Side of Innovation"

Table of contents

1. Introduction

Depending on the industry and competitive environment, innovation and thus creativity can be crucial for company success, so that the question remains how a company can improve its innovativeness.

This paper examines four research studies and four Harvard Business School case studies, in order to discuss this question. Herby the concentration is on the effects of leadership and the relationship between supervisor and subordinate on innovation and/or creativity.

2. Presentation of research and case studies

Research Studies

A company could exploit great benefits if employees voice their ideas, information, and opinions about work improvements. The research study of **Botero and Van Dyne** examines the influence of the individual cultural value orientation of power distance (PD) and Leader-Member-Exchange quality (LMX, quality of supervisor-subordinate relationships) in an organization on employees' voice behavior. They hypothesize that LMX is positively (H1) and PD is negatively (H2) related to Voice Behavior and that PD will moderate the LMX – Voice Behavior relationship (H3), so that PD will make more of a difference in voice when LMX is high. To validate these three hypothesis, two studies were conducted, one in the US and one in Columbia, where the Power Distance is a little bit higher. The result was that both cases confirmed hypothesis 1 and 2. Hypothesis 3 was confirmed in the U.S., however in Columbia the interaction of LMX and PD could not have been confirmed. The final implications of these findings are that high-quality relationships enhance voice and thus positive organizational and individual outcomes. Another main implication for me is that in the U.S., high LMX was only positively related to voice when PD was low. Thus managers should communicate in ways that enhance perceptions of trust while diminishing status differences in order to increase employee voice.

In the next study by **Jung et al.**, examines how companies' innovativeness is being influenced by a top managers transformational leadership (i.e. a leadership style encompassing five components; charisma, idealized influence, inspirational motivation, intellectual stimulation, and individualized consideration), while additionally considering the following moderators for transformational leadership: organizational culture, structure, and the external environment. After surveying managers of 50 Taiwanese companies [1], the positive effects of the transformational leadership, the organizational structure (low formalization, low centralization)

---

[1] From the electronic and telecommunication industry.

and the environment (high uncertainty and high competition) have been confirmed. Also the positive effect of the cultural factor of a higher level of support for innovation has as well been validated. Contradicting to the hypothesis however, a high level of empowerment revealed a negative effect. For me the main results here are the importance of fitting managers' leadership behaviors to the attributes of the organizational context or even seek for changes in those.

Furthermore the study by **Rego et al.** analyzes the influence of authentic leadership[2] on employee creativity. It hypothesizes that an authentic leader promotes creativity indirectly via encouraging employees' psychological capital (i.e. confidence, optimism, hope and resilience) and directly through other mechanisms (e.g. high quality LMX). After questioning 201 supervisors and subordinates of 33 Portuguese organizations, all hypothesis of this study have been empirically validated. The main implication here is that an authentic leader can encourage creativity and thus innovation.

The study by **Murphy and Ensher** is about the leadership style of television directors in order to examine the importance of a charismatic leader, concerning how they improve team's work and creativity. For this study, 21 qualitative interviews with these directors have been conducted, focusing on six behavioral factors of a charismatic leader (strategic visioning and communication behavior, sensitivity to the environment, unconventional behavior, personal risk, sensitivity to organizational members' needs, and deviation from the status quo). The result was that these leaders used these six behaviors to enhance creativity and cooperation among team members. Murphy and Ensher then conclude that the charismatic leadership style can be a way of managing and improving an individual's and/or team's creative potential.

Case Studies
The case study **"Pina Bausch: Leadership as collective genius"** is about Pina Bausch's life, achievements and innovative leadership style. Born 1940 in Solingen, Germany, Pina started dancing at a fairly young age. She later went to the famous New York City dance academy Juilliard School and in 1973 she became the director of dance at the theater of Wuppertal, where she had full creative freedom. She revived the dance theatre by disrupting former dance conventions and thus redefining modern dance, which brought her a lot of attention. She developed new performances and incorporated the ideas of her dancers. Her leadership style can be described as being very respectful, open minded, non-judgmental and democratic

---

[2] Behavior that attracts/promotes positive psychological capacities and a positive ethical climate, thus fostering greater self-awareness, an internalized moral perspective, balanced processing of information, and relational transparency on the part of leaders working with followers, fostering positive self-development (Walumbwa, Avolio, Gardner, Wernsing, & Peterson, 2008).

(treating all equally), inspirational and supportive making everyone feel appreciated and encouraged. She also had a very trustful, close and long relationship to her artists.

The case study **"Luca de Meo at Volkswagen Group"** is about the Italian marketing genius Luca de Meo and his achievements and his leadership style at Volkswagen. De Meo started his automotive career in the 1990's as a product manager at Renault. He then went on to work for several further car manufacturers in ever-higher positions in the marketing departments, until he joined Volkswagen passenger cars in 2009 as the Head of Marketing. Until 2012 he helped VW to improve its *Interbrand* brand-value ranking by 16 places, through different contributions like the Think Blue. initiative, increased collaborations between the international marketing departments[3] or creating smaller, dedicated teams for car launches. His leadership style is being described as being supportive when it comes to going new ways, being more creative, free-thinking or risk-taking and he granted his subordinates a lot of freedom in their work. Additionally he worked with his employees on a very personal und trustful level, having face-to-face talks with over 100 people after his first month at VW.

The case study **"Design Thinking and Innovation at Apple" (2010)**, is about Apple and how the company managed to become one of the most valuable companies of all times and the huge impact the founder and former CEO Steve Jobs had on the success. Apple was operating in many different industries (personal computer, music, cell phones and retail operations), and the premise has always been that the product has to be functional, interactive and especially simple ("Simplicity is the ultimate sophistication" (Thomke & Feinberg 2010, p.3) and with a focus on details. Other crucial criteria of their success where; exact market timing, a great platform strategy and customer involvement. The leadership style of Steve Jobs that is being displayed can be described as authoritarian and inspiring visionary, who gets involved in the innovative process himself and contributes with a great sense of design.

In the case study "**Managing a global team: Greg James at Sun Microsystems, Inc.**", the managerial challenges of a globally spread out team are being discussed. Members are working in different time zones, which leads to a very complicated working situation and cultural misunderstandings. The problem was being examined by the manager after the system went down two times with rather severe consequences and the sub-teams ending up in blaming each other. Underlying interpersonal problems between the team members arose of the feel of unevenness considering the vacation days, distribution of favored tasks, the compensation and the manager's appreciation, sympathy and face-to-face contact, so that the global team that

---

[3] i.e. the Marketing Worx! workshop or the Marketing Round Table.

was supposed to be one, behaved like many separate ones. As a result of this situation, the manager succeeds to improve the situation by increasing the interaction between himself and the team as well as between the teams through for example regular meetings.

3. Discussion of personal conclusions and practical implications

The above described research and case studies show how significant the leadership style and the relationship between the leader and its subordinates can be for organizational success.

My personal conclusion out of these studies will be that the right leadership style or quality of Leader-Member-Exchange to improve innovation and creativity is strongly dependent on different parameters like the organizational and cultural context, as well as the industry a company belongs to. Just like Jung et al. said; it is important to fit managers' leadership behaviors to the attributes of the organizational context.

First of all, it is fairly hard or even impossible to determine one general style of leadership that is most suitable for the improvement of innovation. In the case of Pina Bausch, who can be described as a charismatic leader, it was clear that her style of leadership contributed to the big success of the theatre through a clear communication of her vision and through getting the most out of the dancers by paying close attention to their individual needs, fostering individuals' strengths and taking personal risks. This evidently confirms the results out of the Murphy and Ensher study. She also had a high quality LMX and at the same time a rather low PD. The working environment in a theatre can furthermore be described as art-related (i.e. low-tech). Similar results we can observe from the case of Luca de Meo, a leader that can be described as transformational. He had a very positive impact on the organizational innovativeness through his inspiring motivation and charisma. Furthermore he quickly established high quality LMX (over one hundred face-to-face talks) and an environment of low PD (individual consideration, wearing sneakers and jeans or working door-to-door with lower level employees). Although working in an automotive company, the work environment and activities of the marketing department can be described as low-tech.

On the contrary we have the high-tech case of Apple and Steve Jobs. Here the leadership style is quite hard to define, showing signs of a charismatic (e.g. unconventional behavior or deviation from the status quo), transformational (e.g. inspirational motivation), authentic (e.g. confidence) as well as authoritarian (e.g. dictating policies or taking full control). And yet he had one of the greatest impact on organizational success, taking the company from a basically assured bankruptcy to being one of the most valuable companies of all times. Considering his very authoritarian behavior, Steve Jobs created and organizational culture of a rather high PD.

However, the study also emphasized his personal involvement in the innovative processes, implying a high quality LMX. In the case of Sun Microsystems, the failure of the teamwork was basically the result of the low LMX (except in the USA team), because the manager had very little chance to actually learn about the different problems within the team. After increasing the LMX quality, significant improvements in voice behavior could be seen. The work environment here can be described as high-tech.

Furthermore I reviewed the case studies with a focus on Botero and Van Dyne's implication that (at least in the U.S.) a high LMX only has a positive effect when PD was low. Looking at the cases of Pina Bausch or Luca de Meo, this seems to be confirmed. However, after reviewing the case of Apple, where we can find high LMX yet also high PD, the implication seems to be challenged. One factor for the different result could be the difference in the work environment, with Pina Bausch and Luca de Meo working in a no-/low-tech and Steve Jobs clearly in a high-tech industry.

My further personal result out of the cases and research studies (e.g. Botero and Van Dyne or Rego et al.) is that a high quality LMX is generally in all cases one of the most crucial factors for a successful leadership.

Concluding it can be said that there is a high correlation between the scientific world and real life examples. This underlines the importance of further research in these areas, especially with regard to an increasingly innovation-driven competitive environment.

4. References

Research Studies

Botero, I. C., & Van Dyne, L. (2009). Employee voice behavior: Interactive effects of LMX and power distance in the United States and Colombia. Management Communication Quarterly, 23, 84-104.

Jung, D., Wu, A., & Chow, C. W. (2008). Towards understanding the direct and indirect effects of CEOs' transformational leadership on firm innovation. Leadership Quarterly, 19, 582-594.

Murphy, S. E., & Ensher, E. A. (2008). A qualitative analysis of charismatic leadership in creative teams: The case of television directors. Leadership

Rego, A., Sousa, F., Marques, C., & Pina e Cunha, M. (2012). Authentic leadership promoting employees' psychological capital and creativity. Journal of Business Research, 65, 429-437.

Walumbwa FO, Avolio BJ, Gardner WL, Wernsing TS, Peterson SJ. Authentic leadership: Development and validation of a theory-based measure. Journal of Management 2008

Case Studies

Hill, L. A., Teppert, D. M. (2013). Luca de Meo at Volkswagen Group. Boston: Harvard Business Publishing.

Lange, K. (2012). Pina Bausch: Leadership as collective genius. Berlin: ESMT European School of Management and Technology.

Neely, T., Delong, T.J. (2009). Managing A Global Team: Greg James At Sun Microsystems. Harvard Business School, 9-409-003.

Thomke, S., Feinberg, B. (2010). Design Thinking and Innovation at Apple. Boston: Harvard Business Publishing.